The
Solar
System

The Moon

The Solar System

Contents

Words in **bold** can be found in the glossary on page 24.

©2016
Book Life
King's Lynn
Norfolk PE30 4LS

ISBN: 978-1-910512-86-9

Written by:
Gemma McMullen
Edited by:
Grace Jones
Designed by:
Matt Rumbelow
Ian McMullen

A catalogue record for this book is available from the British Library.

The Solar System

The Sun

The Solar System is the Sun and all of the objects that **orbit**, or go around, it. Eight planets orbit the Sun, including our home, Earth.

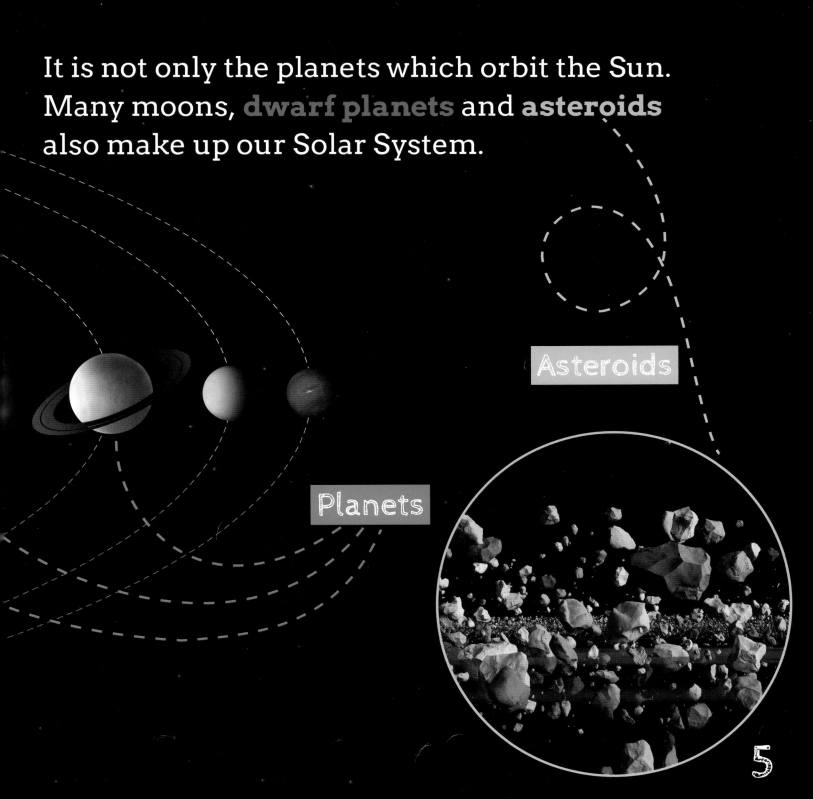

It is not only the planets which orbit the Sun. Many moons, **dwarf planets** and **asteroids** also make up our Solar System.

Asteroids

Planets

What is the Moon?

The Moon is a large ball of rock which orbits planet Earth. It is smaller than Earth, about one quarter of its size.

The Moon has a dusty and bumpy surface. Lots of rocks move around in space. Sometimes they crash into the moon and cause craters.

A crater is a large dent.

The Moon looks white from Earth, but it is grey.

Our Moon

The Moon is the only moon to our planet, Earth. The Moon orbits Earth and Earth orbits the Sun. It takes the Moon around 28 days to orbit planet Earth.

On planet Earth, living things breathe air. There is no air on the Moon so there are no living things.

The Moon's Light

When the Moon is out at night time, it lights up the sky. The light of the Moon is very bright, but the light is not coming from the Moon itself.

The Moon does not give out light. It appears bright because the light of the sun shines on it then back down to Earth.

Other Planets with Moons

Planet Earth is not the only planet which has a moon. Mars has two moons of its own, Uranus has around 27 moons, and both Saturn and Jupiter have over 50 moons each!

Mars

Moons

Uranus

Miranda   Ariel   Umbriel   Titania   Oberon

Our moon is round, but not all moons are the same shape. Many of the moons have been given names by scientists.

Solar Eclipse

Sometimes the Moon moves in front of the Sun. This is called a solar eclipse. As the Sun's light and heat is being blocked, Earth becomes cold and dark for a short time.

During a solar eclipse, animals get ready to go to sleep because they think that night time is coming.

Astronauts

Astronauts are the scientists who learn about space. Astronauts are also able to visit space in special **vehicles** called space shuttles. The first space shuttles ever made were called rockets.

Space Shuttle

Astronauts spend a long time practising what it will be like in space before they travel. Lots of their training is done in water.

Being under water feels similar to being in space.

Visiting the Moon

Astronauts have landed on the Moon before.
A man called Neil Armstrong was the first.
In total, 12 men have walked on the Moon.

The astronauts had to wear special suits when they walked on the Moon. The suits kept them at the right temperature. They also gave them **oxygen** to breathe because the moon has no air.

Why does the Moon Change Shape?

The Moon is always the shape of a ball, but it can look like different shapes in the sky. Sometimes it looks very round, but sometimes it looks very thin.

The shape of the Moon seems to change as it orbits Earth and the sun shines on it. The cycle takes around 28 days.

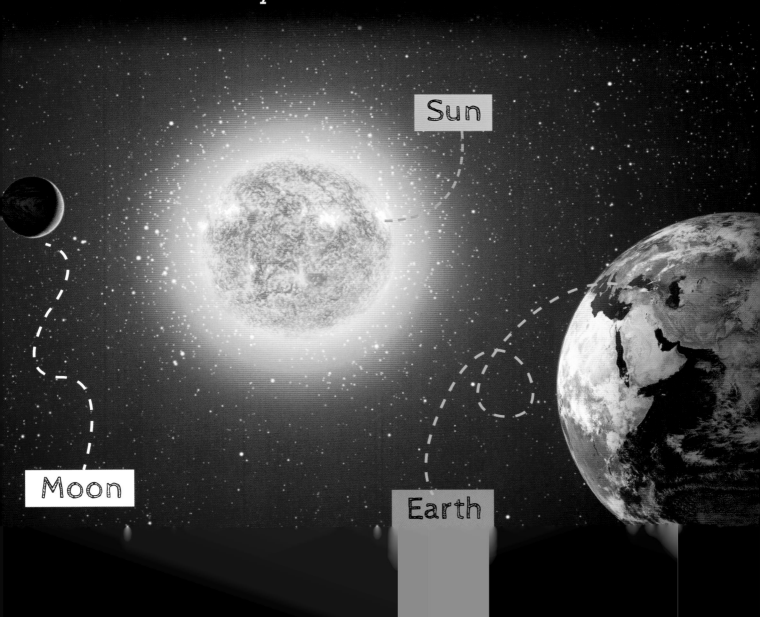

Magnificent Moon!

1 Footprints left on the moon by visiting astronauts are still there.

2 The Romans called the moon Luna.

 The Ancient Greeks called the moon, Selene.

 The moon is very hot during the day but very cold at night.

Glossary

asteroids:	large rocks which orbit the sun
dwarf planets:	very small planets
orbit:	move around
oxygen:	the type of air that humans need to breathe
vehicles:	a thing used for transporting people or goods

Index

Photo Credits

Photocredits: Abbreviations: l-left, r-right, b-bottom, t-top, c-centre, m-middle. All images are courtesy of Shutterstock.com.
Front Cover, 6 6 – Suppakij1017. 1 – Ricardo Reitmeyer. 2-3, 14 – Igor Zh. 4-5 – fluidworkshop. 5inset – Denis_A. 7 – godrick. 8 – MarcelClemens. 9 – HelenField. 10, 21 – Triff. 11 – sdecoret. 12 – Aaron Rutten. 13 – robin2. 15 – Sylvie Bouchard. 16 – 3Dsculptor. 17 – Pavel L Photo and Video. 18 – Aphelleon. 19 – iurii. 20 – mejnak. 22t – Yuriy Kulik. 22br – Nejron. 23tl – Anastasios71. 23b – Romolo Tavani.